REFLECTIONS

A 31 Day Devotional for Women

Valerie Zahn

Reflections: A 31 Day Devotional for Women

© 2022 by Valerie Zahn

Scripture quotations marked KJV are taken from the Holy Bible King James Version.

Scripture quotations taken from the Amplified® Bible (AMP),
Copyright © 2015 by The Lockman Foundation
Used by permission. www.Lockman.org"

"Joy comes in the Morning" by Jessy Dixon/ Gaither Vocal Band Composed by Bill Gaither/ Gloria Gaither/ William J. Gaither/ Public Domain.

All rights reserved. This book or any portion thereof may not be reproduced or used in any manner whatsoever without the express written permission of the publisher except for the use of brief quotations in a book review.

CONTENTS

Title Page
Day 1: God's Way — 1
Day 2: Trust — 3
Day 3: Hiding — 5
Day 4: Masterpiece — 7
Day 5: Genie in the Sky — 9
Day 6: Made in God's Image — 11
Day 7: I am Listening — 13
Day 8: Only One — 15
Day 9: Carrots or Candy Bars — 17
Day 10: Waiting — 19
Day 11: Old Chair — 21
Day 12: Never Give Up — 23
Day 13: Trust — 25
Day 14: He's in the Small Things — 27
Day 15: Glimpses of God in Creation — 29
Day 16: Eternity — 31
Day 17: Sin — 33
Day 18: God's Embrace — 36

Day 19: Testimony	39
Day 20: Dealing with Stress	41
Day 21: Hold On	45
Day 22: Why	49
Day 23: Love and Sacrifice	51
Day 24: Overcoming Fear	53
Day 25: Control	56
Day 26: Names	58
Day 27: Sitting at Jesus' feet	60
Day 28: The voice of His children	62
Day 29: Not Understanding Suffering	64
Day 30: Childlike Comprehension	67
Day 31: God's Love	69
Invitation	73
To My Readers	77
Special Thanks	79
About The Author	81
Books By This Author	83

DAY 1: GOD'S WAY

"For My thoughts are not your thoughts, Nor are your ways My ways, declares the LORD. For as the heavens are higher than the earth, So are My ways higher than your ways and My thoughts higher than your thoughts." Isaiah 55:8-9 (Amplified, Bible)

One day I was folding laundry. With four children at the time, I did several loads a week. I've gotten reasonably good at it. My younger daughter, Keilah, who was three years old, took a towel out of my hand mid-fold and said, "no, no, mommy let me show you how to do it." She takes it and rolls it up into a complete mess. She then takes several other articles from the laundry basket and does the same thing while schooling me on the "right way" to do it.

I thought this was what I do with God. I take

parts of my life out of His hands and believe I can do a better job. I may even tell Him how He needs to fix these areas in my life. Needless to say, my way isn't the best. When things are done my way, it always turns into a rolled-up mess every time.

Thank God for his incredible patience and grace. He comes behind me the same way I did with Keilah, refolds and takes my mess, and makes it right. He does not give up on me. He keeps working with me until I finally learn.

Is there something in your life that you keep taking back from God's hand and making a mess of instead of letting Him be God and doing it right the first time? Let us be challenged today to admit that He knows best in all things even when it doesn't seem right or we think we can do better. He loves you dearly. You can trust Him!

DAY 2: TRUST

"And Moses said unto the people, Fear ye not, stand still, and see the salvation of the LORD, which he will shew to you to day: for the Egyptians whom ye have seen to day, ye shall see them again no more forever. The LORD shall fight for you, and ye shall hold your peace." Exodus 14:13-14 (KJV)

Is there a situation in your life that keeps you awake at night? Is there something that is causing you to fear or worry? Have you done everything you know to do on your part in line with obedience to God? Still, you find yourself wondering what now? I am reminded of the Israelites. They had followed God out of Egypt to the very spot where He had led them to find their enemy (Pharaoh) and the Egyptian army pinning them into a hopeless and impossible situation. When they cried out to Him, He told them that all they needed to do was to stand there and not be afraid and watch what He would do.

When we fear, we do not have faith. When we do not have faith, we are not truly trusting God. The Lord was the one delivering them and doing the work. All they had to do was to trust Him. He had already proven to them time and again that He would provide and protect them.

Whatever the situation robbing you of your peace today, remember what God told the Israelites. Don't be afraid. Trust Him even though trust is challenging in a world and a time when it's hard to trust anyone. You can trust Him. He has proven Himself to you repeatedly. He will never fail you. Now, embrace His peace as He fights for you.

DAY 3: HIDING

"Am I a God who is at hand, says the LORD, And not a God far away? Can anyone hide himself in secret places So that I cannot see him? says the Lord. Do I not fill heaven and earth? says the LORD." Jeremiah 23:23-24 (Amplified, Bible)

One day, I couldn't find my three-year-old son Kamryn. I looked all over my house for him, and he wouldn't respond when I called his name. After only a few minutes, I discovered him under the kitchen table. He had a mouth full of chocolate candy and several wrappers surrounding him. I was angry. What made me mad was the fact that he hid. He hid because he knew what he was doing was wrong, yet he did it anyway.

Are there any areas in our lives that we hide from a pastor or leadership in our church? Perhaps we are hiding things from certain family members or friends? It may not be a sin that we are hiding. Maybe it's something we are struggling with, and yet we put on a smile like everything is fine. If there is any area in our lives that we are hiding, we should examine ourselves. I would dare say that most things we hide aren't' t good. We cannot hide from God. He knows what those areas are, and yet He still loves us. He doesn't want us to clean it up or work it out alone but with and for us. So let's let Him. Surrender whatever it is to Him. Let's live lives where we have nothing to hide, lives of transparency. That is one of the many freedoms we are offered when we have a relationship with Jesus. After all, His opinion of us should be what matters the most.

DAY 4: MASTERPIECE

"For we are His workmanship [His own master work, a work of art], created in Christ Jesus [reborn from above-spiritually transformed, renewed, ready to be used] for good works, which God prepared [for us] beforehand [taking paths which He set], so that we would walk in them [living the good life which He prearranged and made ready for us]." Ephesians 2:10 (Amplified, Bible)

My older daughter, Grace, was two years old at the time. She was playing dress up. I said, "Grace, you are so beautiful. How did you get so beautiful?" she shrugged her little shoulders and said, "God painted me that way."

The world tries to show us what we should look like, the kind of clothes and make-up we should wear, what success looks like, etc... Most of the images and standards we are held up to are fake and are impossible to achieve for anyone. But the God who made the blue sky, the ocean, the mountains, and all the beautiful things in creation also made you just the way you are. You are more special to Him than you can ever imagine. He created you for a specific purpose. It's a plan only meant for you. So, let us stop listening to a broken world that tells us who and what we should be and what we should look like. Let us find our worth in the one who created us for something so much bigger, something special. Just be who He painted you to be.

DAY 5: GENIE IN THE SKY

"For it is by grace [God's remarkable compassion and favor drawing you to Christ] that you have been saved [actually delivered from judgement and given eternal life] through faith. And this [salvation] is not of yourselves [not through your own effort], but it is the [undeserved, gracious] gift of God; not as a result of [your] works [nor your attempts to keep the Law], so that no one will [be able to] boast or take credit in any way [for his salvation]. Ephesians 2:8-9 (Amplified, Bible)

Here are a few of the lyrics of a song I wrote several years ago:

> Who is He to you
> Is He the one that you pray to
> or is He some genie in the sky
> you make a wish to every day and night

> Does He get the glory when He should
> Or just the blame when life's not good
> Who is He to you
> He wants to be your everything
> The lover in the song you sing

We sometimes tend to treat God as a big genie in the sky. He's there to fix all our problems and do whatever we need. We often think we can do our good deeds and then we should get whatever we ask for. But that couldn't be further from the truth.

Through God's grace we receive what we do not deserve (salvation and eternal life with Him). Through God's mercy we do not receive what we do deserve (separation from God due to our sin). We could never do enough good to deserve anything from God. Our good deeds do not earn us salvation. It's His unmerited love. He doesn't want our good deeds; He wants us. All of us! The good, the bad, and the ugly. It's about relationship, not exchanges.

DAY 6: MADE IN GOD'S IMAGE

"So God created man in His own image, in the image and likeness of God He created him; male and female He created them." Genesis 1:27 (Amplified, Bible)

It's easy to see people by social status, race, class, etc. It's things we all get judged for, and we all loathe and speak out against it when given the opportunity. It's easy to like people with the same standards, views, and goals as we do. However, when they don't, we tend to be judgmental. We close people off. Some have been known to 'cancel.' We cannot please God with these kinds of mindsets. We are to love as Christ did. It didn't matter where people were from. It didn't matter how much money they had or didn't have. It didn't matter what garbage was in their past. He loved everyone regardless of any of it. We can love the same way! I believe it starts with remembering that we are all God's creation. We are all made in His image! The person you like and the person you don't. The person who agrees with you and the one who doesn't. Concerning the people we know who are living in sin and aren't yet believers, we must remember Romans 2:4, which says that it's God's kindness that leads to repentance. We can be kind and yet stand firm on God's truth. So, let us put our differences aside and love people for what they are, God's beautiful creation.

DAY 7: I AM LISTENING

"So Eli said to Samuel, "Go, lie down, and it shall be that if He calls you, you shall say, 'Speak, Lord, for Your servant is listening." 1 Samuel 3:9

This past week my husband and I were meeting with our small group at church. For the ice breaker question, the group leader asked, "where did you see God's fingerprints throughout your past week?" I liked my husband's response. He said that answering that question alone should take up the entire time. I thought, wow! That is so true! When the children of Israel were wandering for forty years, the Lord provided manna for them each day. It would spoil if they tried to save more than they needed and for the next day, except for the Sabbath. He was trying to teach them that He would provide what they needed daily. When Jesus taught the disciples how to pray, He said, "give us this day our daily bread."

While both examples were about the need for food being met, I also believe they have a dual purpose and mean spiritual nourishment as well. I believe the Lord wants to teach us and reveal a characteristic about Himself daily. We miss out on a lot simply because we aren't looking or listening. We are distracted by our phones, social media, and Netflix. None of those things are bad, but they can be a diversion to keep us from finding spiritual nuggets. My challenge for us today is to intentionally look for these moments and write them down. Think about how God could use it to impact your children, grandchildren, or someone else.

DAY 8: ONLY ONE

"He who did not spare [even] His own Son, but gave Him up for us all, how will He not also, along with Him, graciously give us all things?" Romans 8:32 (Amplified. Bible)

What is your favorite story in the Bible? Is it David and Goliath? Daniel and the lion's den? Perhaps the miracles of Jesus? A favorite of many is when Jesus was so exhausted that He fell so deeply asleep on a boat. He was unaware and sleeping through a terrible storm while the disciples truly feared for their lives. They woke Him up, and He rebuked the wind, and there was peace. The storm was stilled. My favorite story in the Bible is what immediately took place after. Jesus delivered a demon-possessed man who had been in torment for years living in isolation and complete hopelessness. Knowing who Jesus was, the demons begged to be cast into a bunch of pigs. He granted their request, and the pigs ran and fell off a cliff. After witnessing this, the people who lived in that area asked for Jesus to leave, and He did.

Being a romance author, you probably thought my favorite story would be the story of Esther or Ruth. Maybe Hosea? So, with all the wonderful stories in the Bible, why would this one be my favorite? This is why. Jesus was so exhausted that He was sleeping through being tossed around, loud thunder and lightning, and probably shouting. Yet, He was on His way for (Matthew records it as two men and Mark and Luke one man), not a multitude. Only one or two. As weary as He was, as difficult as the journey, He was willing to go out of His way for only one. You and I are also that one. Our heavenly father didn't even spare His one and only son for you; Jesus willingly went to the cross and suffered for you. Be encouraged today, knowing just how special you truly are. You are that one.

DAY 9: CARROTS OR CANDY BARS

"For the time being no discipline brings joy, but seems sad and painful; yet to those who have been trained by it, afterwards it yields the peaceful fruit of righteousness [right standing with God and a lifestyle and attitude that seeks conformity to God's will and purpose.]"
Hebrews 12:11 (Amplified, Bible)

I love how God gives us metaphors and glimpses of spiritual truths illustrated in the physical realm. One of those examples, I believe, is food. With the help of advertising, we crave foods that aren't good for us, such as fried, processed foods, and foods loaded with sugar. Consuming these foods keeps us from looking our best and feeling our best and can even cause premature death. I don't know about you, but when I eat these types of foods (which I do more than I should), I'm usually not satisfied and want more junk food and not healthy foods that I should eat.

Whereas healthy food is more brutal at times to put down. It requires more discipline. It requires training our pallets to want it instead of unhealthy food. However, when we do eat healthy food, we have more energy. We feel better about ourselves and look better. Ultimately it can prolong our lives and give us a better quality of life.

Eating unhealthy food stems from instant gratification as opposed to healthy food that you eat and wait on the superior results. The same is true of sin versus living a life of obedience to the Lord. As we flip through the channels or see billboards on our way to work, we are bombarded with images that pull us and draw us into sin. Sin, like junk food, leaves us feeling bad about ourselves and unsatisfied and can lead to death and separation from God.

Today, let us be challenged to make the harder choices. We need to train and disciple ourselves in the things of God. It's the only way to experience the fullness of life that God has intended for us to have.

DAY 10: WAITING

"Wait for and confidently expect the Lord; Be strong and let your heart take courage; Yes, wait for and confidently expect the Lord." Psalm 27:14 (Amplified, Bible)

I don't know about you, but waiting is one of my biggest challenges. Whether it's waiting on God to answer a prayer, waiting on the call from the doctor, waiting on that exciting package to arrive, or waiting on that slow person in line. Whether we're waiting on something potentially scary, frustrating, or wonderful, waiting is difficult.

However, even though God knows it's hard, He set things up that way. We have to wait on a lot of things. We plant, we wait, we harvest. We conceive, we wait, and there's new life. I will repeat it. Waiting is hard! So why does God make it so necessary? I asked my twelve-year-old daughter her thoughts on this. She said it's to help us get patience. I agree with her. Patience, after all, is a fruit of the Spirit. I believe it also causes us to learn to rely on Him and teaches us to trust Him. It can also cause us to be grateful. If there were no waiting, we would be lacking. What are some reasons you think God causes us to wait? I feel there are many. Whatever the reason, or reasons, I know it is for our good. So, the next time you find yourself waiting, try focusing on the beauty of the process.

Some of the best parts of life are the excitement of waiting. When the thing we are waiting for finally does come, it's over, and then we are quickly waiting on the next thing. Let's not wish our lives away, dreading what might come next, and get frustrated in the waiting. But rather see God in the process. Let's try and focus more on what He's trying to teach us to make us more like Him.

DAY 11: OLD CHAIR

"Do not judge by appearances [superficially and arrogantly], but judge fairly and righteously." John 7:24 (Amplified, Bible)

We have this old rocking chair in our younger boys' room. It's brown. It has some stains on it. It doesn't rock too well anymore. When it does, it makes a terrible sound. I've learned that lifting my left foot while rocking a certain way rocks smoother, and there's no sound. I still rock my youngest in it. I'm sure by now you're wondering, "why are you holding on to this piece of junk?"

So, I will tell you. My parents bought this chair fourteen years ago before my first child was born. This chair has rocked all six of my children to sleep multiple times. Four of my children were rocked in this chair by my late dad. While some may view this as trash, my heart still regards it as treasure.

We, as humans, tend to judge and discard things and people based on appearances, and although that isn't always bad, at times, it can be. We often look at others and their things and label them or make them feel of less worth. Some may even judge me for having such a terrible chair. This causes me to think of the fact that it's not uncommon for young people to misunderstand the worth of older people who have more experience and wisdom. On the other hand, it's not unusual for older people to misunderstand the value of younger people by not seeing their gifts, talents, and potential.

Let us all be challenged not to judge on appearances and realize we all have worth and value. And to answer your question, yes, I will eventually get rid of the chair.

DAY 12: NEVER GIVE UP

"Be unceasing and persistent in prayer; in every situation [no matter what the circumstances] be thankful and continually give thanks to God; for this is the will of God for you in Christ Jesus." 1 Thessalonians 5:17-18 (Amplified, Bible)

My grandmother once told me how she had worried and prayed for her dad to be saved for many years. She tried to talk to him about Jesus, but he was completely shut off from anything regarding Christianity. One day, not long before he died, he was listening to the radio. A preacher came on. This time, he chose to listen instead of turning it off. He said the minister made a lot of sense. So, after he listened, he knelt on his knees and gave his heart and life to Jesus.

When he was on his death bed, the family surrounded his bed moments before he died. He looked at them and said, "Don't cry for me. In just a few minutes, I will be walking the streets of gold." What if my grandmother had stopped praying for him?

Let me ask you, is there someone you have been praying for for a long time? You may be the only one in the world praying for them. I want to encourage you never to give up!

DAY 13: TRUST

"He called a little child and set him before them, and said, I assure you and most solemnly say to you, unless you repent [that is, change your inner self-your old way of thinking, live changed lives] and become like children [trusting, humble, and forgiving], you will never enter the kingdom of heaven."
Matthew 18:3 (Amplified, Bible)

Jesus makes it clear that we must become like little children to enter heaven. So, what does that mean? Children can be very temperamental. They often find it hard to share and get along with others. They whine when they don't get their way. They can be extremely selfish and unreasonable. I could go on and on. But if we are being honest, are they not much diffcrent than us? They just haven't yet learned how to mask their feelings and actions like adults.

So, what qualities does Jesus want us to have

like little children? I have six children. I am by no means an expert on them, but I do have a little experience. My children never worry about their needs ever being met. They know that they are always going to have meals and snacks. They are always going to have clothes and shelter. My children don't worry about tomorrow. They don't worry about something terrible happening to them. Why? It's not because we are these fantastic parents, but because children trust their parents and caretakers.

This is not the only point that Jesus is making about becoming like little children, but I feel like it is one of them. There is no better daddy than our heavenly one. He has and always will provide for all our needs. He will protect us from all harm. So why, dear sisters, do we not trust him at times? Why do we worry about so many of our tomorrows?

I think it all comes down to trust. I genuinely feel like our Lord wants us to be at liberty to enjoy this gift of life He's given us, trusting Him with our every need and desire as dear little children.

DAY 14: HE'S IN THE SMALL THINGS

"Delight yourself in the LORD, And He will give you the desires and petitions of your heart. Commit your way to the LORD; Trust in Him also and He will do it." Psalms 37:4 (Amplified, Bible)

I was in college at the time; I decided to go shopping on a Saturday morning. While walking through the store, I passed by various flowers for sale. I spotted the most beautiful lilac rose. Lilac is my favorite color. I wished such a rose would be given to me. Almost as quickly as I had that thought, I dismissed it. I had recently come out of a very unhealthy relationship. Being in another one was a terrifying thought. I went on my way, enjoyed the rest of my day, and never gave the rose a second thought.

That evening, one of my good friends was going on a date with her boyfriend. I was glad to have the night all to myself. Out of nowhere, I got a call to come down to the dorm lobby. When I walked out, my good friend was standing beside her boyfriend. She was holding a dozen pink roses, her favorite kind. I was confused as to why they had called me down. Then suddenly, my friend's boyfriend pulled out the most beautiful single lilac rose I had ever seen. It was even more beautiful than the one I had seen earlier that day. He said when he saw it, it reminded him of me. He felt compelled to buy it.

No one knew about what happened earlier that day except God and me. It was my God flower. He saw the desire of my heart. I love how God is in the details. He doesn't just care about the big things but the small things as well. Ask yourself and give it some deep thought. Where do you see God in the details of your life?

DAY 15: GLIMPSES OF GOD IN CREATION

"For ever since the creation of the world His invisible attributes, His eternal power and divine nature, have been clearly seen, being understood through His workmanship [all His creation, the wonderful things that He has made], so that they [who fail to believe and trust in Him] are without excuse and without defense." Romans 1:20 (Amplified, Bible)

As I have mentioned in a previous devotional, I love how God reveals characteristics about Himself in creation. In my book "I'll See You on Friday," the main character Abigail, mentions she loves the ocean. The reason is it reminds her of God. She says, "It's so powerful and mysterious yet peaceful and beautiful. It can be terrifying and yet calm."

The sun also reminds us of God. It's so powerful nothing can survive if it gets too close. It's so bright we can't look straight at it, or we can go blind. It's the most powerful source of energy we have. It sustains all life.

There are so many glimpses of spiritual truths illustrated in the natural. I want to challenge us today. Look around. What are some other things in this world that show glimpses of God? Who He is? His power? Even though sin has corrupted this world, there are still so many beautiful truths to be seen.

DAY 16: ETERNITY

"For ALL FLESH IS LIKE GRASS, AND ALL ITS GLORY LIKE THE FLOWER OF GRASS. THE GRASS WITHERS AND THE FLOWER FALLS OFF, BUT THE WORD OF THE LORD ENDURES FOREVER." And this is the word [the good news of salvation which was preached to you." 1 Peter 1:24-25 (Amplified, Bible)

Last summer, my husband and I took the family to the beach for vacation. The ocean was too choppy on one particular day, and no one could get into the water. Trying to make the most of our day, we went to a gas station, bought the largest Icey's they had, and walked the beach. We walked as far as possible before reaching part of a military base. It was so enjoyable. As I reflect on that day, it was one of my favorite memories from the entire trip.

As we walked back, I had the children stop walking for a few minutes, pick up one tiny grain of sand, and hold it. When they did, I explained to them how our life is similar to this tiny grain of sand, whether you live a long or short life. The decisions we make and the way we live is significant. Every decision and choice we make in this tiny period will affect eternity. This tiny grain of sand is like your lifetime compared to all the grains of sand on this entire beach and beyond.

It's a daunting thought. We only have a limited time to give our lives to Jesus and live in obedience to Him. When we get to heaven, we will be with Him and naturally do good. Here, however, it's not natural but a moment-by-moment choice and sometimes a sacrifice. So, let's be challenged to make the most of this day, and every day after, with the time we have because it impacts our eternity.

DAY 17: SIN

"When we were living in the flesh [trapped by sin], the sinful passions, which were awakened by [that which] the Law [identifies as sin], were at work in our body to bear fruit for death [since the willingness to sin led to death and separations from God]. But now we have been released from the Law and its penalty, having died [through Christ] to that by which we were held captive, so that we serve [God] in the newness of the Spirit and not in the oldness of the letter [of the Law]" Romans 7:5-6 (Amplified, Bible)

Several years ago, my grandmother was diagnosed with liver cancer. As soon as she found out, she started trying to do things that would get rid of it, but it was too late. It had already taken over, and nothing could be done. She died three months later.

I started thinking about how cancer is very

similar to sin. If not addressed as soon as it's found, it can spread quickly and cause eternal death. This also had me thinking about others. I don't know about you, but as a Christian, it's always been difficult to understand how we're supposed to love everyone, hate the sin, and love the sinner. But it was hard for me to understand exactly what that looks like. How do you do this when people's lifestyles are contrary to what God wants, yet they don't care? They despise you for not being ok with doing what is wrong.

The best way I know how to deal with it is to think of people in such lifestyles as full of cancer. If this cancer isn't dealt with, it will eventually take their life...their enteral life. To me, this is so sad, and it grieves me. Instead of being angry or disgusted with them, we should feel overwhelming compassion. As with anyone with cancer, we should persistently pray for them. We should never be ok with their condition. But out of deep love and empathy, try to help them get the ultimate healing they need from the great physician, Jesus. We should cover them with overwhelming love, kindness, and prayer. We should follow in the steps of our Savior.

After all, the sinners came to love Jesus because

of His great love for them. It was the religious people who put Him on the cross. So, let's be challenged today to deal with the sin in our lives so that it never spreads or takes over. Also, let's love people as Jesus loved with genuine concern and deep compassion!

DAY 18: GOD'S EMBRACE

"This is My commandment, that you love and unselfishly seek the best for one another, just as I have loved you." John 15:12 (Amplified, Bible)

In 2018 my dad was suffering terribly from bone cancer. My mom and I brought him to the doctor's office for a chemo treatment. He was so critical that the doctor wanted to have him admitted to the hospital. We had waited a long time. My mother-in-law, sister-in-law, and her family were on their way to come and stay for the week for their spring break. I had several things that I needed to get done before their arrival. My mom kept urging me to go home and take care of the things, and she would call me when she needed me. After more persistence, urging, and time, I decided to go home.

DAY 18: GOD'S EMBRACE | 37

Broken-hearted, I walked into my house and began to prepare for my guests. My husband was working from home and had been with our four children. When he saw the sadness on my face, he pulled me into his arms and held me firmly in his embrace. While he was holding me, I heard the Lord clearly say that He was holding me. He was using my husband's arms to do it. I said with tears, "Lord, what about my mom? Who is going to hold her?" He responded that He was taking care of it.

Within minutes my phone rang. It was my mom sobbing. She asked if I could come back. My dad had been moved into a room. I left immediately and headed to the hospital. After I got there and my dad was settled in, my mom and I sat down. I told her what had happened earlier, what God had said to me, and how He had used my husband to hold me, and He said He would hold her too.

As soon as those words left my lips, my mother began to weep. After a couple of minutes, she pulled herself together and told me that just before she had called me, she was talking with one of the hospital staff at a desk. In the middle of their conversation, she broke down crying. The lady behind the desk walked around to my mother, wrapped her arms around her, and held her tightly. God had used this woman to comfort my mother. As I write this, I realize that this woman may or may not have known how God used her to impact our lives that day, but what an impact she made.

There is a big world out there with many hurting people of all colors, backgrounds, and ages. Let us be challenged today to let God use our arms, hands, smiles, money, and everything we have for HIM. After all, our gifts and belongings have been given to us for His glory and others' good.

DAY 19: TESTIMONY

"I will tell of your name to my countrymen; In the midst of the congregation I will praise You." Psalms 22:22 (Amplified, Bible)

"The one who believes in the Son of God [who adheres to, trusts in, and relies confidently on Him as Savior] has the testimony within himself [because he can speak authoritatively about Christ from his own personal experience]. The one who does not believe God [in this way] has made Him [out to be] a liar, because he has not believed in the evidence that God has given regarding His Son." 1 John 5:10 (Amplified, Bible)

Take a moment and think about your life. Think about the ups and downs and all that has transpired in your walk with the Lord that makes you who you are today. What is your testimony? The beauty of your story or testimony is that no one can take it away from you. It's what has molded you into the person you are and how you see and process the world around you. Another wonderful thing about a testimony is that it's not over as long as you're breathing.

Testimonies aren't experiences we are meant to hide, even if there's a rough start before the happy ending. They are intended to be shared for the benefit and encouragement of others. Testimonies are for others to know if God did something like that for you; he could also do that for them.

Some of you might be thinking that you don't have much of a testimony. It's not too late to change that. God is in each and every moment of your day, desiring your attention and fellowship. He's in the details. You just have to be open to see what He's doing. It's up to you and me to choose to set aside time and moments to see Him, converse with Him, and be still and know He is God."

DAY 20: DEALING WITH STRESS

"Casting all your cares [all your anxieties, all your worries, and all your concerns, once and for all] on Him, for He cares about you [with deepest affection, and watches over you very carefully]. 1 Peter 5:7 (Amplified, Bible)

We all have multiple things in our lives that cause stress, such as bills, jobs, family conflict, etc... Throughout our days, we have several things that pop up that can cause stress like traffic, being late, drama from our children, and you fill in the blank. I think it's safe to say that stressors are inevitable and impossible to avoid.

As we also know, stress is very unhealthy for us. It's proven to cause high blood pressure, heart problems, asthma, diabetes, headaches, depression, and so on. If stress is inevitable and is toxic for us, why do we have to experience it?

The answer to that question is that we were never intended to. We were supposed to have lived forever in a beautiful garden of paradise that had everything we would ever need. There in that garden, we were to enjoy a close relationship with God and simply enjoy Him and His magnificent creation. However, when sin entered the world, it changed everything. So now, we have those annoying things and situations that cause us STRESS.

So as Christians, how do we deal with stress? As a homeschooling mother of six, I have in no way mastered this ability. But I can tell you what works for me. First, we must acknowledge that we are made up of mind, body, and spirit. It's not a one thing fixes all. So, let's talk about the mind. Philippians 4:8 (KJV) says, *"Finally, brethren, whatsoever things are true, whatsoever things are honest, whatsoever things are just, whatsoever things are pure, whatsoever things are lovely, whatsoever things are of good report; if there be any virtue, and if there be any praise, think on these things."* Whatever we think about influences our stress level, especially if we are dwelling and thinking about those things that our enemy, satan, always tries to bring to our minds.

Also, one of the best things that have helped me in this area is to be thankful. I heard it once said that you can't be worried and grateful simultaneously. Stop for a second and think about something in your life that is causing you stress. Start thanking God for whatever you can about this situation. You may have to dig deep even if the problem is horrible. Even if all you can say is thank you, God, that you are working this together as a plan for my good because your word says so (Romans 8:28).

Our bodies are another part contributing to our stress levels. We must give our bodies what they need to feel and function properly. When we are hungry and tired, we aren't going to deal with adverse situations well. Our bodies need vitamins, hydration, exercise, and rest. This isn't saying that we need to be fitness models, but we do need to be good stewards of what God has given us and take care of ourselves.

Lastly, satisfying our spiritual needs is the most crucial element of helping with stress. There's a place in every human being that can only be filled and met by God. He is our Creator, and He alone can only perfectly fill that spot. This comes by surrendering our hearts and lives to His bigger plan and purpose and walking in a relationship with Him.

We may not be able to avoid stress, but we do have the ability to make life go a little smoother. Let's be challenged today to not be victims of it but to do our part by preparing our, minds, bodies, and Spirit.

DAY 21: HOLD ON

"For His anger is but for a moment, His favor is for a lifetime. Weeping may endure for a night, but a shout of joy comes in the morning."
Psalms 30:5 (Amplified, Bible)

When I was in high school, I had anorexia. I'm a petite person with a small frame. A good weight for me is a range between 105-107 pounds. A weight I haven't been since my four children were born. Anyway, I got down to around 80 pounds. My parents and friends were very worried about me. I had frequent doctor visits where I was weighed and threatened that if I didn't start eating, I would have to be fed by a tube.

It was indeed one of the darkest times in my life. I experienced absolute oppression and depression. I genuinely felt like I was in a dark hole that was impossible to get out of. I felt as though I would never smile again. I struggled to make it through each day. Back then, getting professional help was seen in a negative light. So, unfortunately, I didn't receive any.

My eating disorder had nothing to do with thinking I was fat or my appearance. The issue I was struggling with was fear and a lack of control over my life. I was expressing negatively that I needed help but not the kind of help that doctors, family, and friends could offer. I needed the healing, love, and compassion only my Savior could give.

The crazy thing about it is that I grew up in a Christian home. I was a Christian. Yet I was broken; I dare say shattered. Suicide was a daily thought. However, my youth pastors taught one Wednesday night that those who commit suicide go to hell. Not knowing if that were true, I didn't go through with the images that frequently played out in my mind. However, in a way, I was doing it by slowly starving myself.

Out of utter desperation, I went to the only source I knew. At the time, I didn't have access to a Christian radio station. I found a cassette tape we had, and I would listen to one of the songs on that tape over and over. The lyrics of the song said: *"Hold on, my child. Joy comes in the morning. The weeping only lasts for the night. Hold on, my child. Joy comes in the morning. The darkest hour means dawn is just in sight."* I began reading chapter after chapter in the Bible. I would pray day and night, crying out to God for the darkness to disappear.

Although this horrible dark time lasted a couple of years, I slowly improved until I was healed. As I slowly let go of control and put this darkness in the hands of the One who is truly in control, the fear went away. Since that miserable time, I have smiled and laughed more than I deserve. I could never have dreamed that God would have given me the life He has. I would be lying if I said that I hadn't experienced dark times since. But what I can honestly say is because of that dark time and experiencing God's goodness and faithfulness during it, it has gotten me through other hard times. I can say with absolute certainty as horrible as that time was, I am genuinely grateful for it, for I wouldn't know God the way I do now.

Even though I didn't receive counseling, I would recommend CHRISTIAN counseling to anyone struggling with an eating disorder or mental or emotional illness. I believe my journey wouldn't have lasted as long as it did if I had gotten Christian counseling. If you are someone who is struggling, know you are not alone. There are so many others out there who are and have struggled just like you. Please reach out and get CHRISTIAN counseling. God's word heals!

I also encourage you to find your song in the night. A song that you can play that will help you get through another day until your healing is manifest. Let the words that once encouraged me also bring encouragement to you. Hold on, my child. The darkest hour means dawn is just in sight.

DAY 22: WHY

"And we know [with great confidence] that God [who is deeply concerned about us] causes all things to work together [as a plan] for good for those who love God, to those who are called according to His plan and purpose." Romans 8:28 (Amplified Bible)

It always surprises me how young children start asking that one-word question when you say no. "Why?" Sometimes, as parents, we may give them an explanation, and other times we may not. They eventually get over it, accept it, and stop asking because they know that we love them and always have what's best for them at heart. They can trust the outcome.

Don't we often do the same thing with God? We often ask Him "why" when something happens that we don't like as if we deserve an explanation. God responds similarly to the way we handle our children. Sometimes we get an explanation, and sometimes we don't. Most often, we see why later. When we look back, we can see we dodged a bullet.

Let us be challenged today to focus on His unfailing matchless love for us. Let's choose to have faith that He knows best. Unlike earthly parents, He knows the future. We can trust that His outcome is what's best for us. He always has what's best for us at heart.

DAY 23: LOVE AND SACRIFICE

"And Jesus replied to him, 'YOU SHALL LOVE THE LORD YOUR GOD WITH ALL YOUR HEART, AND WITH ALL YOUR SOUL, AND WITH ALL YOUR MIND.' This is the first and greatest commandment. The second is like it, 'YOU SHALL LOVE YOUR NEIGHBOR AS YOURSELF [that is, unselfishly seek the best or higher good for others]." Matthew 22:37-39 (Amplified, Bible)

We are required to love God and others, but I think we often forget that genuine love requires sacrifice. Think about a mother's love and all of its sacrifices, such as sleep deprivation, time, energy, money, and doing whatever needs to be done instead of what we want to do. Even while typing this devotional, my two-year-old pushed my chrome book out of my lap because he wanted to sit in it for a total of 1 minute. So, where was I? Oh yeah, SACRIFICE!

What about the love of a spouse or boyfriend? There is the sacrifice of time, energy, compromising your opinion, etc... Jesus gave the ultimate example of the greatest sacrifice. John 15:13 (KJV), "Greater love hath no man than this, that a man lay down his life for his friends."

Genuine love requires sacrifice, and we are to love our neighbor. Let's be challenged today to go out and love people the way God loves us. Let's be willing to sacrifice voicing our opinion for our neighbor, our time, and our money. Let God fill in the blank as to what we need to sacrifice to genuinely love others the way He wants, and the way Jesus demonstrated.

DAY 24: OVERCOMING FEAR

"And my God will liberally supply (fill until full) your every need according to His riches in glory in Christ Jesus." Philippians 4:19 (Amplified, Bible)

When I was around nine or ten, my family went to the Sunday night service at church. This particular night, they didn't have preaching. Instead, they watched a movie about the end times. It absolutely terrified me! I feared that one day I could be left behind. I didn't sleep a wink that night, and that fear lingered with me for years until one day, God revealed something to me that I will share with you. Since then, I haven't worried about it anymore.

Peter had every intention to die for Jesus during His trial and crucifixion. But when the time came for him to prove himself, he couldn't do it. He even cursed and denied knowing Him. However, several years later, Peter did die for Jesus.

So, what changed? Why wasn't he able to do it for Him the first time? He had literally been walking and talking with Jesus face to face for a few years. Why was he able to do it after he hadn't seen Him in years? The answer is the Holy Spirit. The Holy Spirit is the one who gives us the ability and strength to do the impossible. Peter didn't have the power of the Holy Spirit to give him the strength and the ability to do it at that time because the Holy Spirit hadn't been given. Also, it wasn't Peter's time to go home yet. He had a lot more work to do for the Lord. But when it was his time to go home, he had what he needed and could do it. This is why we do not need to fear the future. God provides what we need one day at a time, not days and years in advance. Just like He did for the children of Israel concerning the manna.

After my dad died, my daughter, who was eight years old, began having panic attacks. She would find it hard to breathe and cry, "I don't want to die, I don't want to die." One day I took her on a walk and shared exactly what I just shared with you. She's never had another panic attack since.

Whether you or someone you know is experiencing something similar, be encouraged that there is no need to fear. The Holy Spirit will always provide what you need when you need it.

DAY 25: CONTROL

"And He Himself existed and is before all things, and in Him all things hold together. [His is the controlling, cohesive force of the universe.]" Colossians 1:17 (Amplified, Bible)

One morning my husband brought me a handful of nightlights and said we didn't need that many. I proceeded to cry and be angry with him. When he saw my reaction, he said, "What's wrong? This isn't about nightlights." I started to think about it. He was right. My response was a bit ridiculous. I had put just enough night lights out and spaced them, so I didn't have to turn on a light if I needed to get up. Yet, this had nothing to do with that. It was simply about control.

In a matter of two months, we found out that my dad's cancer was back. This time it wasn't looking good. I woke up each day not knowing if we would have to take him back to the hospital or if he would make it through the day. During this time, our stove went out, we started having septic tank issues and had to get it pumped, and our heating and air conditioning went out and had to be replaced.

I was completely out of control of everything going on in my life. But I could control the number of nightlights and where I placed them. It's completely absurd, I know, but it's a true story. Since then, I've been reminded that even when we feel like we are in control of our lives, we never really are. The truth is that the only thing we are in control of is what thoughts we allow in our minds and how we respond to everything that happens to us.

Let's be challenged today to rest and find comfort in the fact that we know and walk with the One who truly is in control. Even when we live in a world and in a time where it seems there is only chaos, He is and will always be in control, and He's got you!

DAY 26: NAMES

"The name of the Lord is a strong tower; The righteous runs to it and is safe and set on high [far above evil]." Proverbs 18:10 (Amplified, Bible)

What's your name? Have you ever looked up its meaning? Names are important to God. They all have a meaning. An angel told Mary to name her baby Jesus. An angel told Zechariah to name his and Elizabeth's baby John. Also, God changed Abram's name to Abraham and Sarai's name to Sarah. Jesus changed Simon's name to Peter. Those are only a few examples of God changing names to fit His purpose.

We are familiar with a few names of God: Elohim-Creator, El Elyon- the most high God, El Roi- the God who sees, Jehovah Jireh- the Lord provides, and Jehovah Rapha- the God who heals. He is our El Shaddai- all sufficient one. Be encouraged today that no matter what you are going through, He is all you need. He is the "I AM."

DAY 27: SITTING AT JESUS' FEET

"But the Lord replied to her, 'Martha, Martha, you are worried and bothered and anxious about so many things; but only one thing is necessary, for Mary has chosen the good part [that which is to her advantage], which will not be taken away from her." Luke 10:41 & 42 (Amplified, Bible)

One day, during my quiet time with the Lord, He impressed upon me to stop focusing on the ways I want Him to use me and to focus on spending time with Him. Time with Him is what matters most. As I am typing this, I am reminded of Mary and Martha in the Bible. I tend to be more like Martha, a doer, and a planner. I often miss out on God's gifts right in front of me because I'm looking and planning on what's to come. Quite often, I find myself serving in areas only out of guilt. I've missed out on a lot of precious fellowship because I was too busy and not just sitting and being still at Jesus's feet.

Hopefully, you can't relate to this at all, but if so, let's change that today. Let's take time out before we go to bed or have a quiet moment to reflect on God and what He's done for us that day. How we've blown it and how we can learn from it. Let's take time and talk to Him and listen to what He has to say. Let's not miss out on another moment in hearing and having and experiencing all that the Lord has for us.

DAY 28: THE VOICE OF HIS CHILDREN

"FOR THE EYES OF THE LORD ARE [Looking favorably] UPON THE RIGHTEOUS (the upright), AND HIS EARS ARE ATTENTIVE TO THEIR PRAYER (eager to answer), BUT THE FACE OF THE LORD IS AGAINST THOSE WHO PRACTICE EVIL." 1 Peter 3:12 (Amplified, Bible)

"When the righteous cry [for help], the Lord hears and rescues them from all their distress and troubles." Psalms 34:17 (Amplified, Bible)

A few years ago, I was volunteering at our church's VBS. In my class, groups of around sixty children would rotate throughout the morning.

During one of the rotations, amongst all the many little voices, only one stood out to me. I heard, "Mommy." My eyes searched through the crowd, and there was my little son, Micah, with a huge smile on his face.

In that large group of children, all of whom I cared about, only one of them was mine. That made him special and stand out from all the rest. This is a very tiny snapshot of the way it is with God and His world. He loves everyone, but only some are His. They are the ones who look to Him for their provision, protection, love, friendship, etc. Their voices stand out in the sea of voices from around the world.

DAY 29: NOT UNDERSTANDING SUFFERING

"For our momentary, light distress [this passing trouble] is producing for us an eternal weight of glory [a fullness] beyond all measure [surpassing all comparisons, a transcendent splendor and an endless blessedness]!" So we look not at the things which are seen, but at the things which are unseen; for the things which are visible are temporal [just brief and fleeting], but the things which are invisible are everlasting and imperishable." 2 Corinthians 4:17 & 18 (Amplified, Bible)

One night, while praying, I thought of my dad on the final day that he could talk and communicate with us. I thought about how much he suffered. It was horrific. I told God, "I will never understand why you allowed him to suffer as you did."

Even though God gave me no explanation, and He doesn't have to because He's God. He did reveal to me how my dad didn't choose to have cancer and suffer as He did. At any time during his suffering, if he had a way out, he would have taken it like anyone else.

Jesus, on the other hand, had a choice in His suffering, yet He chose to do it. He suffered more than my dad ever did. At any time during His suffering, He could have called down angels, and the anguish would have instantly stopped. But He didn't. He willingly chose to endure every agonizing moment so that when my dad left his suffering, he could run into His arms and never have to suffer again.

I may never understand why my dad and so many others have to go through all that they do. What I do know is that we live in a fallen world. It's not the world God intended for us to live in. He created the garden of Eden, which was supposed to be our home. A world with no sickness, sadness, pain, or death.

After Adam and Eve disobeyed, sin came and ruined everything. Thankfully, God made a way that everything will be as He intended one day. However, until then, we cling to Him.

I will always hold onto and remember when my dad was suffering so severely; I saw him raise his hands as high as he possibly could and praise Jesus. Even though he had to go through it, he wasn't going through it alone. He had a Savior who was familiar with suffering and held him through it all. Now to me, that is a God worth serving!

DAY 30: CHILDLIKE COMPREHENSION

"When I was a child, I talked like a child, I thought like a child, I reasoned like a child; when I became a man, I did away with childish things. For now [in this time of imperfection] we see in a mirror dimly [a blurred reflection, a riddle, an enigma], but then [when the time of perfection comes we will see reality] face to face. Now I know in part [just as fragments], but then I will know fully, just as I have been fully known [by God.]" 1 Corinthians 13:11 & 12 (Amplified, Bible)

My family and I visited my in-laws in IL a few years ago. We were on our way to an amusement-type place for the kiddos. One of the cousins was riding in the car with us. My husband was using GPS because he had never been to the place we were going. When the GPS began to tell him when and where to turn, my youngest daughter, who was around four years old, looked over to her cousin and said, "My daddy's phone talks to the road."

If you are a mother, grandmother, or have been around a child for any length of time, I'm sure you have similar stories you could share. They are so funny and so cute. It doesn't matter how intelligent the child is; their little minds can only process and comprehend so much.

It reminds me of the scripture in *1 Corinthians 13:12 (AMP) that says, "For now [in this time of imperfection] we see in a mirror dimly [a blurred reflection, a riddle, an enigma], but then [when the time of perfection comes, we will see reality] face to face. Now I know in part [just as fragments], but then I will know fully, just as I have been fully known [by God.]"*

Today let's humble ourselves and keep in mind that no matter how old or long we've walked with our Savior, there's no way we can fully process or comprehend the magnificence of God and His truths, and yet we should keep on striving to do so.

DAY 31: GOD'S LOVE

"By this the love of God was displayed in us, in that God has sent His [One and] only begotten Son [the One who is truly unique, the only One of His kind] into the world so that we might live through Him. In this is love, not that we loved God, but that He loved us and sent His Son to be the propitiation [that is, the atoning sacrifice, and the satisfying offering] for our sins [fulfilling God's requirement for justice against sin and placating His wrath]." 1 John 4:9 & 10 (Amplified, Bible)

With all the incredible attributes of God, if I could completely understand and comprehend just one of them, I would choose to understand His love for me. I am convinced if I could truly grasp this, I would sin less, have faith that could move mountains, and never doubt again.

There is no love comparable to His love. Why is it so hard to grasp? I see His love for me in answered prayers. It's shown in the beauty and smell of the flowers and the serenity of the mountains and ocean. It's felt in the embrace of the people I love and the cool breeze of autumn. It's heard in the songs of the birds and the laughter of my children.

It still seems so impossible to comprehend because His love is not from this world, and our comprehension is minimal, as we talked about in the last devotional. Yet, there is still so much that we can experience in this world. We must look for it, remembering that He is in the details. We need to stop and take time to sit at His feet and just let Him love on us.

My prayer for you, dear sister, is Ephesians 3:17-19 (AMP), which says, *"So that Christ may dwell in your hearts through your faith. And may you, having been [deeply] rooted and [securely] grounded in love, be fully capable of comprehending with all the saints (God's people) the width and length and height and depth of His love [fully experiencing that amazing, endless love]; and [that you may come] to know [practically, through personal experience] the love of Christ which far surpasses [mere] knowledge [without experience], that you may be filled up [throughout your being] to all the fullness of God [so that you may have the richest experience of God's presence in your lives, completely filled and flooded with God Himself]."*

INVITATION

As a romance author, I obviously enjoy a good love story. However, the greatest love story ever told starts with the Prince of Heaven who had everything, needed nothing, and yet desired to have a relationship with you. Before you ever knew Him or even cared to know Him, you were on His mind and you continue to be—to the point that He left perfection, trapped Himself into a physical mortal body, and came to this very imperfect world with nothing. He suffered horrifically by being tortured and dying in your place as the sacrifice for your sin and guilt, so that one day you would be able to be with Him in His perfect world when you leave this one—instead of the alternative. He did all of this, just for the possibility that one day you might choose to love Him back. It's what His heart truly desires. Whether you are aware of it or not, He constantly pursues a relationship with you.

However, the ultimate decision is up to you. The love He has for you is far greater than anything you have or ever will experience in this world, and the benefits to this precious relationship don't just begin when you die but as soon as you say yes to His invitation to have a relationship with Him. Instead of fear, despair, and hopelessness, when you accept Jesus as your Savior, you immediately receive peace, joy, and hope. Although we live in a world where bad things happen, He will never leave you or forsake you and will help you through any situation that may come your way. You may ask yourself, "How can I obtain such a treasure?

First, you need to acknowledge and admit that you are a sinner. Like everyone else, you have sinned and aren't perfect, and you need saving. Second, repent of your sins. Confess your sins to God. Be truly sorry for what you have done that is displeasing to God. Third, believe that Jesus Christ, God's only begotten Son, died for your sins, in your place, for your salvation. Fourth, accept God's free gift of salvation through faith in Jesus Christ and His death at the cross for you. Lastly, dedicate your life to Jesus. He not only saves you from an eternity in Hell when you accept Him as your Savior, but He also intercedes for you at all times to God the Father in order to obtain for you God's power in your life to live for Him.

Here's where you stop living for yourself (an empty life that has only left you feeling unsatisfied and always wanting more) and instead start living a life with purpose. Here is where you stop traveling alone on this path that seems to be wandering nowhere and start traveling with Him by your side with a beautiful destination before you—and wow, what a journey!

Will you accept His invitation? Will you make this simple choice, a choice to love the One Who so loves you, by accepting His Son Jesus? I can honestly say that accepting Jesus as my Savior has been the best decision I have ever made. He has seen me through the best and worst of times in my life. From the births and adoptions of my children to the death of my dad. He has been my Rock. He alone truly gives me hope and joy in a world, and in a time, where it seems there is none. He can do the same for you. Will you let Him? This is truly the greatest love story ever told.

TO MY READERS

Thank you so much for taking your precious time to read these devotionals over the past 31 days. I pray that you were blessed and encouraged in some way. I hope and pray that you know just how loved and special you truly are. If you enjoyed this devotional, I would love to hear what you have to say. Please consider leaving a review on Amazon. To find out about current and future books, please visit my website at https://www.valeriezahn.com and consider subscribing to my blog. Thank you again!

SPECIAL THANKS

First, I want to thank God, who has blessed me exceedingly and abundantly above all that I could ask for or think. I am eternally grateful for his pursuit and for never giving up on me. He is my first love and forever will be. Secondly, I want to thank my wonderful husband, Steven. I love and appreciate you more than I can ever express. Thank you for completely supporting and encouraging me along every step in my writing journey.

I also want to thank my amazing children. You are truly a blessing from the Lord. Thank you for your encouragement. I love you with all my heart. Next, I would like to thank my mother Judy, my brother Craig, and my mother-in-law Brenda. This book would not be possible without you. Lastly, I would like to thank my beloved family and friends who have always loved, encouraged, and supported me. I thank God for each of you.

ABOUT THE AUTHOR

Valerie grew up in small southern towns. She was blessed to come from a culture where life revolved around Jesus and family. She always had a vibrant imagination and enjoyed all things media related. As a young adult, she attended Lee University, majoring in telecommunications. After college, she enjoyed a successful career as a video editor. She has worked for both local networks as well as a national entertainment network. During this time, she met and married Steven.

After getting married, she continued working until she was blessed with her first child. After becoming a mother, she found that her heart's desire was to be a stay-at-home mom and wife. Since making that decision, she and Steven have become the proud parents of four biological children and two adopted children from foster care.

While her first love will always be God and her family, she has never lost her passion for crafting an engaging story. She hopes her writing will bring both an escape from the world's daily problems and a testimony of God's goodness, love, and grace.

For more about Valerie's books and giveaways, visit her online at: https://www.valeriezahn.com.

BOOKS BY THIS AUTHOR

I'll See You On Friday

"I'll See you on Friday" is book one in the Unexpected Love series. It was 1918 and the Great War had just ended. After years of uncertainty and loss, the entire nation breathed a collective sigh of relief and began celebrating. Abigail was very thankful, but also found herself feeling restless and in need of purpose. Her fiancé, Luke, had died during the war. She had kept herself busy as a nurse helping the wounded and serving her country. What would she do now?

As the world celebrated, the Queen decided to tour her country and personally thank them for all of their sacrifices. After meeting Abigail, the Queen was very impressed. She invited her to visit the palace to meet her son, Prince Everett. She hoped Abigail would give the Prince a reason to abandon his carefree lifestyle and finally provide both a Princess and heir for the royal family.

After meeting Abigail, the Prince finds out that she

never intends to marry or give her heart to another man. She only wants to live a life of service to others. The Prince strikes up a deal with her. He proposes that they marry legally, in order to appease his parents, while he pursues true love. Abigail would also be able to use her position as Princess in order to serve the nation. However, from the moment they say I do, nothing goes as planned.

No Ordinary Wildflower

"No Ordinary Wildflower" is book two in the Unexpected Love series. Prince Everett and Princess Abigail have enjoyed over twenty years of marital bliss. After receiving tragic news from the palace, their lives will be changed forever. While their marriage is in distress, another problem arises.

Prince Adrien, heir to the throne, has made a decision that could impact both the future of his family as well as the kingdom. With the help of old friends, Abigail attempts to secure the future of both her son and kingdom. As the plan is set in motion it quickly begins to unravel. Torn between love and duty, will Adrien rise to the challenge and prove that he's worthy of the crown?

It's All In His Gaze

"It's All in His Gaze" is the third and final book in the "Unexpected Love" series. After twenty years of marriage, Prince Adrien and Princess Rachel find themselves in a good place. Their love has survived the test of distance, time, and many hardships. As an effort to bring the people of Noreland together, Prince Adrien has taken on the challenge of putting together an art exhibition. Soon after he's too far into this endeavor, he finds out that he will have to work closely with an old flame from his past. Someone that could destroy his marriage and ruin the beautiful life he and Rachel have made together.

Meanwhile, Queen Abigail must rely upon her unshakeable faith more than ever after King Everett receives word of tragedy that throws him into a depression. As he spirals deeper into his grief, it threatens to completely change his character as the husband and father his family has always known and depended upon. He forces his only daughter, Princess Judith, whose heart was set on remaining single, to marry and not just anyone. She must choose a nobleman from a selection of suitors he has picked. Her mind must be made up by the Valentine's Day ball where the engagement will be announced. If it's not, the king will choose for her.

Trying to find solace from a hopeless situation, Princess Judith travels to her sister-in-law's farmhouse in the country. While there, she's reintroduced to an old friend, and a romance is rekindled and set ablaze. However, due to her father's ultimatum, they can't be together.

Will the king come to his senses before it's too late? Will his only daughter be doomed to a life of misery with someone she does not love?

Made in the USA
Monee, IL
29 January 2023